BiBlE MaX

More time with God

GW00705974

Journeys with God

Genesis David Bruce | **Ruth** Helen Warnock

Also in the **Bible Max** series:
What's God like? includes series on John's Gospel by Robert Willoughby and Psalms 1–41 by Elaine Carr.

© Scripture Union 2007
First published 2007

ISBN: 978 1 84427 282 2

Scripture Union, 207–209 Queensway, Bletchley, Milton Keynes, MK2 2EB, England
Email: info@scriptureunion.org.uk
www.scriptureunion.org.uk

Scripture Union Australia, Locked Bag 2, Central Coast Business Centre, NSW 2252
www.scriptureunion.org.au

Scripture Union USA, PO Box 987, Valley Forge, PA 19482
www.scriptureunion.org

British Library Cataloguing-in-Publication Data.
A catalogue record of this book is available from the British Library.

Printed in China by 1010 Printing International Ltd

Cover design by Wild Associates Ltd

Internal page design by Creative Pages: www.creativepages.co.uk

Scripture Union is an international Christian charity working with churches in more than 130 countries providing resources to bring the good news about Jesus Christ to children, young people and families and to encourage them to develop spiritually through the Bible and prayer. As well as coordinating a network of volunteers, staff and associates who run holidays, church-based events and school Christian groups, Scripture Union produces a wide range of publications and supports those who use our resources through training programmes.

CONTENTS

INTRODUCING...

BIBLE MAX

More time with God

The **Bible Max** series aims to help you get the big picture of God's story as you read big chunks of his Word as part of an extended time with God.

Perhaps you have tried using Bible notes which give you a short passage to read each day. But, like lots of people, you may find it hard to keep going with daily Bible-reading times because life is too busy. Shorter passages may not make much sense out of context if you've forgotten what you were reading a few days before. **Bible Max** will help you read and immerse yourself in longer bits of God's Word including whole Bible books.

You might want to use **Bible Max** for longer regular reading, setting aside half an hour or more every so often. Or, you might use it for special times away from every day commitments, for example, on holiday, days off or even for a retreat day. Although the material is written mainly with individuals in mind, you may also enjoy using it with others. But it's not just a question of knowing more about the Bible. **Bible Max** means spending more time with God. Each session offers suggestions and questions to help you talk with and grow in your relationship with him.

'The big picture' introduces each series, giving you some idea of where the Bible book fits into the big picture of the Bible and God's big story. Then there are several reading sessions with suggestions to help you into the Bible passages and to reflect on how it might connect with your own life today. Each series concludes with 'Bird's eye view' – a section to help you reflect on what you've read and then think about what it might mean for you. There's also lots of space for your own journaling as you're reading, where you can make a note of things God is saying to you – if you like to do this.

Different section headings are there to help you through each session with the Bible material. But don't feel you need to stick with the order suggested. Pick and choose what's helpful for you. Miss out a section, read more, read less! Relax – and see where God leads you as you spend time with him.

JOURNEYS WITH GOD

Journeys with God includes two series – one on Genesis and one on the book of Ruth. **Genesis: beginnings** helps us think about the beginning of the journey of God's people and their early travels with him. **Ruth: a journey with God** looks more intimately at the life journey of one individual. The two Bible books are different in their styles and purpose and this is reflected in the different approaches taken by the writers.

As you read, reflect and pray, our prayer is that you will be greatly encouraged as you discover more about what God is like and grow in your relationship with him.

We'd love to hear how you get on with *Bible Max*. Please email us at: biblemax@scriptureunion.org.uk

About the writers…

David Bruce is Director of the Presbyterian Church in Ireland's Board of Mission. He was formerly Regional Secretary for Scripture Union in Britain and Ireland.

Helen Warnock is General Director of Scripture Union Northern Ireland. She has a background in youth work and is passionate about helping others get to know God and engage with him through the Bible.

GENESIS: BEGINNINGS

The Big Picture

The word Genesis means 'origin'. Traditionally considered to be one of the books of Moses, it's not surprising that the author should want to describe the beginnings of the world and the people who lived in it. It's also the beginning of the big story of God's relationship with humanity which continues through the whole of the Bible.

Who do you think the book of Genesis is for? Rich people? Poor people? Insiders? Outsiders? You and your friends? This story is for everyone. Many of the stories in Genesis involve violence, the break-up of families and the uprooting of people from all that is familiar to them. Sometimes the 'heroes' don't behave very well. Many of the characters embark on journeys which involve moving from place to place and, in the process, making major discoveries about themselves and God.

As you read Genesis, try to be aware of your own journey with God. Be ready to learn more about him and what he wants to teach you as you read.

BiBle Max

There are many different journeys within Genesis. The map here shows the two major ones. Later, God would lead his people out of Egypt (Exodus) and into the Promised Land (Joshua).

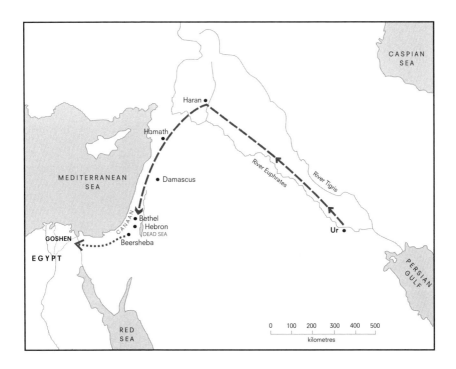

c1925 BC Abraham and his family journey from Ur to Canaan.

c1700 BC Jacob and his sons journey from Canaan to Egypt.

c1280 BC Moses and the people journey out of Egypt.

c1240 BC Joshua and the people journey into the Promised Land.

There is debate amongst scholars about the actual dates – these give a rough idea of the possible timings.

GETTING STARTED

What are your hopes as you launch out on this journey with *Bible Max* in Genesis? Here are some questions to start you get thinking about this. You might like to jot down any thoughts in the journal space below.

Why have you decided to read the Bible?

What are your hopes as you start out?

Do you *expect* that God will speak to you?

If so, have you any idea what might he say?

Genesis 1–11 includes the creation of the world and describes the lives of its earliest human inhabitants: Adam and Eve; Cain and Abel; Noah and his family, and the flood which destroyed everything and ushered in a new beginning.

Genesis 12–36 tells the story of the early ancestors of the Hebrew people: father (Abraham), son (Isaac) and grandson (Jacob). The sons (and grandsons) of Jacob – later renamed 'Israel' – would become the leaders of the twelve tribes of Israel.

Genesis 37–50 is the life story of Joseph, one of Jacob's sons. Joseph is the reason that the family decamp and journey to Egypt where they will remain for over four centuries. It's from this point that Exodus picks up the thread with the extraordinary story of Moses' journey and his bold bid for freedom beyond the desert.

THINK ABOUT...

Where might you find yourself in the stories in Genesis?

How do you think the book of Genesis might be relevant to you and your life today?

What questions do you have as you begin your reading of this book?

Write your thoughts in the space below. You might like to talk with God about these now.

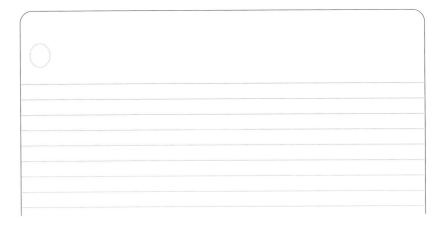

1 Beginnings: from nothing to everything

GET READY

Where did we come from? Where are we going? Why do we exist? Do we have any significance beyond our presence here and now? Jot any thoughts down in the space below.

READ Genesis 1–3

Pretend that you have picked up the Bible for the very first time and started to read at page one. As you read Genesis 1–3 now, try to approach it as if you have never seen it before. Try to forget what you think you know or assume about God. Ask yourself this important question as you read: What kind of God is described here?

This should take about fifteen minutes, so make yourself comfortable. You might find it helpful to note down thoughts as they occur in the journal space. Use the thought-starters below if that helps.

God creates…	God commands…
God acts…	God blesses…
God makes…	God is…
God gives…	

BiBlE
MaX

INTO THE BIBLE

Hebrew poets loved parallels, repeating patterns to emphasise an idea or theme. Look back over Chapter 1 and notice these:

Days one and four (1:3,14): light into darkness; sun and moon.

Days two and five (1:6,20): sea and sky; fish and birds.

Days three and six (1:9,24): dry land; creatures to inhabit it.

The sixth day of creation is the culmination – God makes humankind in his image (1:26,27). No matter how people choose to understand the mechanics of creation, it happened.

There were limits to what the man and the woman could do in the garden God had made for them.

Read Genesis 2:16,17 again. Now, look away from the text. What are the strongest impressions you have been left with by these two verses? Circle the phrase or phrases below that come closest:

'you must not eat' (v 17)	'the tree of the knowledge of good and evil' (v 17)	'you will surely die' (v 17)	'you are free to eat from any tree in the garden' (v 16)

What does each phrase suggest about God's character?

Read again the conversation between the snake and the woman (3:1–5). Does Eve add any restrictions to God's original instructions to Adam about the garden (see 2:16,17)? What do you think the woman understood about God?

GOD AND YOU

- What is it about God's character that strikes you most from this story of creation?

- Think about some aspects of his creation which particularly inspire you. What do they tell us about our Creator and his concern for us?

- How would you describe Adam's relationship with God? How did that change when he and Eve disobeyed God (3:8–10)? Think about your own relationship with God now. Are you eager to meet with him, or wanting to hide?

- Some people today say that to seek significance in a relationship with a 'god' is delusional. But many others see definite signs of where God has been at work in their lives. Write down two or three major moments in your life where you have seen God at work.

- Think about these chapters in the light of what Jesus has done for you (eg John 3:16). Praise him.

INTO ACTION

Think back over the story of the Fall in chapter 3. Have you given in to temptation? Is there sin to confess? Wrongs to put right? Take time to talk with God about this. Ask for his forgiveness if you need to, and for strength to put things right.

God's creation was 'good' (eg Genesis 1:10,25). How have people spoilt it? Genesis 1:28 suggests that we have a responsibility to care for the world God has made. How are you doing this now? Are there ways in which you could work with others to do more?

2 Cain and Abel: rejection and acceptance

GET READY

The story of Cain and Abel is about rejection and acceptance. Do you feel that God has accepted you? If you have doubts about this, why do you think this is? What kinds of people does God accept? Does he 'reject' anyone?

READ Genesis 4,5

These chapters contain a sad story. The first person to be born was a murderer. As you read, look for signs of God's blessing on the world and God's curse on it. If you like, make a note of these in the journal space.

Extra

It's possible that Cain and Abel were twins. The firstborn was in a more favourable position, even in these earliest days. There is a hint of this in the names given to the brothers at their birth. The word 'Cain' means 'possession'. There may be some wordplay in Eve's delighted exclamation: 'With the help of the LORD I have brought forth [or 'have acquired'] a man' (4:1). 'Abel' by contrast means 'breath' or 'vapour', and Eve says virtually nothing about him or his birth. It seems that compared with her firstborn, Abel is an afterthought.

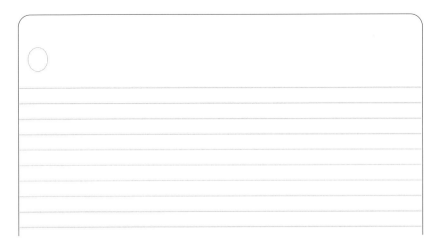

INTO THE BIBLE

Look again at the story of the births of Cain and Abel (4:1,2). How are these births described? Who gets most attention?

What careers do the two brothers pursue? Verses 3–5 describe the offerings the two brothers brought to God. How was Cain's promising start in life turned on its head? Why was an awful family tragedy the result?

Why do you think Cain's offering was rejected (v 5)? Could there be a clue in Genesis 3:17–19? God had told Cain's father, Adam, that, as a result of sin, the ground would be cursed and that only hard, physical work would bring food. Could Cain's great efforts show he is looking in the wrong place to find a way back to God and the Garden of Eden from which his parents had been banned?

Why do you think Abel's offering of a firstborn lamb was accepted (v 4)? Might Genesis 3:21, where God himself covers the fallen Adam and Eve with garments of skin, give us a clue?

What might the long genealogy in chapter 5 tell us about God's presence and purposes? Look especially at verses 1, 2, 22–24 and 29. Look out for some of the same names in the genealogy in Luke 3:23–38.

GOD AND YOU

- What was the sin that was 'crouching' at Cain's door, that desired to have him and which he failed to master (v 7)? Unspeakable evil acts can be provoked by everyday emotions. To what 'sins' are you in danger of falling prey? Talk with God about danger areas in your own life. Is there jealousy, anger or disappointment which, if not mastered, could lead to disaster?

- Do you ever feel rejected by God? Think again about what gives you certain knowledge that you are accepted by him (eg Hebrews 10:19–22).

- Take a look at what Hebrews 11:4 says about Abel. How far are you trying to win God's approval through your own efforts? How far are you trusting in God?

- Read again the verses about Enoch (5:18–24, see also Hebrews 11:5). How closely are you walking with God (v 24)?

INTO ACTION

Take time to identify and write down the emotions you have felt most keenly when mistakes have been made in the past. Do these emotions still feature in your life? Who is master of them? Ask God for his help in this.

Are there family rivalries in your life? How might you take action to put things right?

3 Noah: from ridicule to rescue

GET READY

What do you know about Noah's story? As you read, think about what parts of the story might be lost if we treat it as a cartoon or children's adventure.

READ Genesis 6–10

This is a lengthy section – but don't be put off by that! Chapters 6–9 tell the story with the words that the Lord spoke quoted verbatim throughout. If you are looking at this with another person or a group, you might like to read it aloud, but have a different voice reading the narration.

Hearing a story often associated with children told by adult voices and for adult ears may help you hear this familiar story in fresh ways.

INTO THE BIBLE

Genesis 6:1–7 Some of this is puzzling. The phrase 'sons of God' (vs 2,4) usually means angels in the Bible, while the Nephilim or giants (v 4) who populated the earth were clearly outside God's design. Read again Genesis 6:5–7. Whatever the exact meaning, people had overreached themselves and God judged them.

How was Noah different from others in his society? Look out in these chapters for all the ways in which we see his faithfulness to God.

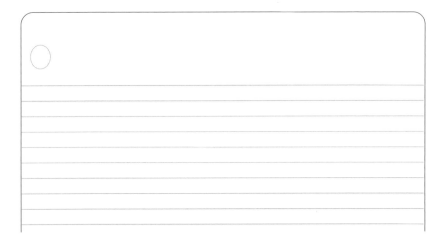

BiBlE Max

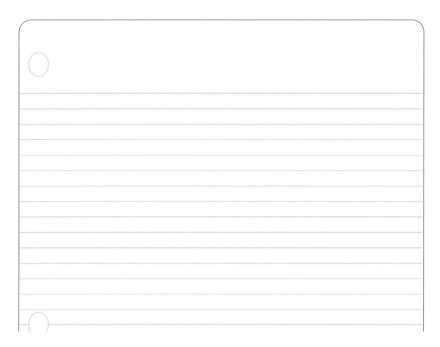

Genesis 7,8 Judgement falls, and through the water that saves the occupants of the floating ark, the rest of life is destroyed. Look for the signs in this story of extraordinary grace and terrible judgement acting together.

Genesis 9:1–3 How does what God says to Noah here differ from his words to Adam (1:28,29)?

Genesis 9:8–17 What is the 'covenant' that God establishes with Noah?

GOD AND YOU

- Think of some parallels between the days of Noah and our own time. How do you think God might bring judgement into these circumstances?

- The apostle Peter likens the waters of this flood to the waters of baptism (1 Peter 3:20,21). As Christians we believe that Jesus has both taken God's judgement and saved us through his death and resurrection. Take some time to praise him for what he has done for you.

- Read chapters 6,7 again looking out for the emphasis on Noah's obedience to God and his faith in him. How far do obedience to God and faith in him characterise your life at the moment?

- Write down the questions you would like to ask Jesus about his Father's actions in destroying the world this way.

- Noah was a godly man whose binge-drinking session (9:20–29) leaves him incapable and vulnerable. Ham's reaction abuses and undermines his father; Shem and Japheth take respectful action. What is your reaction to the weaknesses of others?

Extra

Ham's shameful abuse of his father's exposure alienates him and his descendants from the rest of the family. The Canaanites (Ham's descendants, 9:18) would forever be in opposition to God's ways.

INTO ACTION

Psalm 46 describes how God is our refuge and strength, even though the waters of the sea 'roar and foam' (Psalm 46:3). It can't be easy to have faith in a good God when he seems to be invisible, as many of the victims of great natural disasters must have felt (eg the Asian tsunami).

Talk this over with God. We may struggle with the wholesale suffering in this story, and we need to tell God this. Be ready, by faith, to be content with the partial vision we have been given.

Turn this puzzlement into prayer for people who are facing a disaster. Log on to www.tearfund.org/praying for up-to-date news on world situations – and use this as a prompt for your prayers.

4 Abram: called to a new home

GET READY

Choose a different Bible version from the one you usually use to read these chapters. Try Eugene Peterson's *The Message* or the New Living Translation. The story races along. Follow the story on the map (page 7), or use a Bible Atlas for more detail.

READ Genesis 11–16

As the various family dramas unfold, try to imagine how Sarai and Abram would have felt in the hardest moments of each crisis.

INTO THE BIBLE

How does the story move from Noah to Abram? Trace Abram's journey from Ur (11:31) to Hebron (13:18).

Abram was the head of a nomadic tribal family, loosely settled in Haran (11:31). God's promise to him (12:2,3) must have seemed very surprising indeed and unlikely. What was the promise?

After the trip to Egypt, the family returns to Canaan and settles in Hebron. Abram becomes caught up in a civil conflict between local rulers, culminating in the kidnap of Abram's nephew Lot at Sodom (14:12). Why was Lot living in Sodom? What do you think motivates Abram to rescue Lot? Can you imagine the conversation between Lot and Abram after the rescue is completed?

Look out for the ways in which Abram shows his trust in and obedience to God. Now look back over the chapters and notice where Abram's faith failed.

GOD AND YOU

- Can you find yourself, or situations you know, in these stories? Can you see God's hand at work helping you? Perhaps there is something you'd like to pray about.

- Read these chapters again. What can you work out about the kind of person Abram was? What was his relationship with God like? Are you like Abram in any ways? What could you learn from him to help you grow in your own relationship with God?

- **Genesis 14:18–20** There is a mystery in these verses. Who is Melchizedek, King of Salem (later to be 'Jerusalem'), priest of God Most High? The victory celebrations include a blessing from him to which Abram responds by tithing his possessions. The writer of Hebrews speaks about Jesus being a priest for ever in the order of Melchizedek. Read Hebrews 7 now, and spend some time reflecting on the work of Christ as our high priest.

- Abram was already an old man (even by post-flood Genesis standards) when he set out from Haran. What spiritual ambitions do you have for your old age?

- Abram has doubts that lead him to make rash decisions. The elderly Abram and Sarai must have wondered how God intended to make a nation from their non-existent offspring (15:2–5). Sarai's maid Hagar is invited to help things along (16:1,2). Think of some times when you've been tempted to take control of events yourself rather than waiting on God. Perhaps you're in such a time now. Ask God to help you keep trusting him.

Extra

> Although Ishmael was later estranged from his father (21:8–21) he would become the ancestor of the Arab peoples and is revered today as a prophet in Islam.

INTO ACTION

Is God calling you to do something new for him? What is it? Ask him to help you take the first step of obedience.

Think about the various family relationships and tensions you've read about in these chapters. What do you find hardest about being part of a family? Being a parent? Uncle or aunt? Someone's child? Pray about any difficult issues in your family life. Ask God to help you take action if needed.

5 Promises: from Abram to Abraham

GET READY

Most families have some skeletons in the cupboard – things we would rather weren't talked about, or told to others. Some of the characters and incidents in Genesis 17–20 might fall into this category! The good news is that God's story is bigger than ours – so he can do remarkable things with us, our families and our futures.

READ Genesis 17–20

In your reading, pause between each chapter. In the pauses, write down your reactions to the chapter you have just read. Feel free to record surprise, shock, anger, wonder, excitement, puzzlement or unanswered questions.

INTO THE BIBLE

As you read and journal, try to respond to the characters in each story. What would they have been like as colleagues or family members of yours? Would you have liked them? Respected them? Understood their reactions?

If these chapters were a soap opera, what title would you give to each episode?

Genesis 17 What was the 'covenant' God made with Abraham? And what was the significance of his and Sarah's changed names (vs 5,15)?

Genesis 18 Abraham and Sarah had three visitors. Who do you think they were (vs 10,17)?

Genesis 19 Trace Lot's sad story through this chapter. Look back to chapter 13 to remind yourself why he was living in Sodom. His family life collapses, not only with the death of his wife, but through the misguided foolishness of his daughters (vs 30–38).

Genesis 20 How does the story of Abraham and Abimelech show that Abraham had not learnt earlier lessons (Genesis 12:10–20)?

Extra

Andrei Rublev, a fifteenth century Russian Orthodox iconographer, understood the three visitors to represent God the Father, Son and Spirit. You can find an image of Rublev's icon of the Trinity by searching on Google (www.google.co.uk).

GOD AND YOU

- Genesis 17:7 speaks of God establishing an everlasting covenant with Abraham's descendants. Through Christ, this includes us. Think of three words that describe your relationship with God – if you like, write them in the journal space. How do these words connect with God making an everlasting promise to be your God?

- In Genesis 18 the Lord speaks to Sarah and Abraham through the three visitors. Whoever they were, at the very least we must say that God was tangibly present with Abraham and Sarah that day. Would you say that God is 'visiting' you in any way at this point in your life? How does this happen?

- Abraham pleads for Sodom and Gomorrah, growing with boldness each time he reframes his questions. Did he stop too soon? Would God have relented from destroying the cities because Abraham asked him, and because he loved the people? What does this say about the power and purpose of prayer? How persistent are you in praying for others?

INTO ACTION

Disobedience, foolishness and the mistakes that follow need not be the last word on a person's life. Take a moment to thank God that, with him, failure is not final. If you feel comfortable doing so, write down the story of how this has proved to be true for you.

Is there a difficult situation that you are very concerned about (eg personal, family, society, international)? Spend some time interceding on behalf of those involved and asking God to bring some answers to that situation.

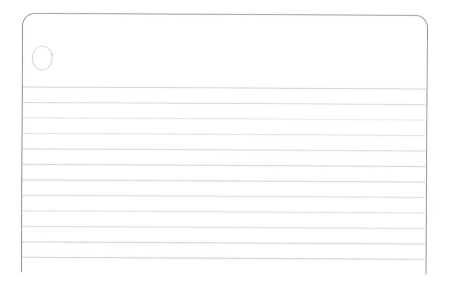

BiBle Max

6 Isaac: testing times

GET READY

Take time to think back over your life, and that of your parents and grandparents. Each person will have had different experiences of God. Each generation will have had different high points and low points. In a sentence or two, try to write the story of ways in which God has been real to different generations of your family.

READ Genesis 21:1 – 28:9

This is a longer reading – think of it as a short biography of Isaac. There are various threads in the story which will be easier to keep in mind if you read it all at one sitting. If you are doing this with others, it might help if everyone reads it before coming together.

INTO THE BIBLE

Genesis 21:1–21 Isaac and his half-brother, Ishmael, go their separate ways (21:8–20). How does God deal with both the parents and their two sons?

Genesis 22:1–19 In this amazing story where Abraham comes close to sacrificing his son, what parallels can you see with Christ's sacrifice for us? What makes it particularly amazing that Abraham was prepared to obey God in this? Look at Hebrews 11:17–19 for some clues.

Genesis 24 Imagine yourself in the place of Abraham's servant. How would you have told the story of your journey to find a wife for Isaac?

Genesis 26 Look out for the ways in which Isaac repeats the mistakes of his father, Abraham.

Genesis 27 is a twisted story of deceit and double-dealing. Where do your sympathies lie? Why do you think God allows this deception to happen?

Think about similarities between this story and Cain and Abel. Esau (the firstborn) has the place of privilege and his father (Isaac) has the place of power. Jacob and his mother are second class and powerless. Yet God has made a promise that the elder son will serve the younger (25:23). God blesses Jacob and Rebekah as they address their powerlessness in the only way they can. In Chapter 28 Jacob is affirmed as the father of the continuing people of God's promise.

GOD AND YOU

- Abraham acted in faith in his willingness to sacrifice his son. Genesis 22:5 suggests that he was confident Isaac would return with him alive. The writer to the Hebrews celebrates his faith (Hebrews 11:17–19). How strong is your faith in God when you can't see where he is leading?

- Isaac and Rebekah were 'grieved' by their son Esau and his wives (26:35; 28:8,9). Why do you think this was? Think about and pray for parents who are grieving for their children today.

- Look again at how Isaac repeats the foolish mistakes made by his father with Abimelech (Genesis 26). What might help prevent us from repeating the mistakes of those who have gone before us?

- God works through flawed people – like Jacob. In spite of your flaws, how might God be wanting to work through you?

INTO ACTION

God seems to have a bias towards the underdog (eg Deuteronomy 10:18). Can you identify individuals or groups who might be seen as marginalised, or second class in our society, and think of how God views them? Write down some words to describe this. What might you do to model God's compassion for them?

Isaac's life had many testing times. Bring some of your own challenges to God now and ask for his wisdom in facing them.

7 Jacob: journey with God

GET READY

Are you curious about your human ancestry? Many people have discovered a greater sense of how they fit in to the world by knowing something of their past family history. These chapters take us on a journey from Bethel to Mizpah – and, along the way, Jacob's family line is established.

READ Genesis 29–31

Start by rereading chapter 28:10–22, and then continue until the end of chapter 31. As you read, fill in the blanks on the family tree below to show the children of Laban's daughters, Leah and Rachel, and their servants, Zilpah and Bilhah.

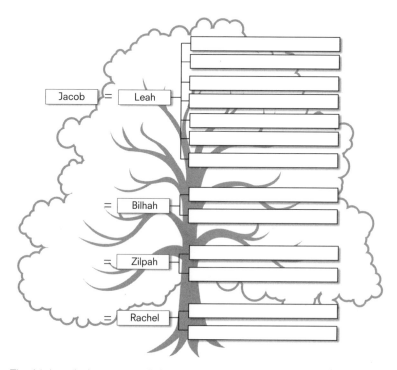

The births of eleven out of the twelve sons of Jacob are recorded in these chapters. The twelfth son, Benjamin, was born to Rachel at the moment of her death (35:18).

INTO THE BIBLE

What words would you use to describe the relationship between the two sisters, Leah and Rachel? If you knew Jacob personally today, would you admire him? What would you like or dislike about him?

Look for the twisted motives in these stories:

How does Laban get more work from Jacob (29:26,27)?

How does Rachel get even with her sister (30:1–9)?

How does Jacob gain wealth and influence over Laban (30:31–43)?

Jacob is drawn back to his homeland (31:3) – the theatre for God's dealings with his people. For Jacob and his descendants the land was crucially important, and remains so today. Jacob also established holy places as markers of special times. Bethel (28:10–22) and Mizpah (31:45–55) would have powerful memories associated with them. What was their significance?

GOD AND YOU

- Reflect for a moment on how God might view these incidents in the life of Jacob and his family. How does he use them? Think of some surprising ways in which God has worked through circumstances in your own family's life. Can you see how God is in control of everything?

- Think of Jacob's special meeting with God at Bethel (28:10–22). Can you identify places or times that have been significant in your own spiritual life? What special moments, decisions or commitments in your journey with God do these remind you of?

INTO ACTION

Jacob's story is full of contradictions. God used him in amazing ways, but his life was inconsistent. At times he was as twisted as his name suggests (27:36), but at other times he was faithful and acted with integrity.

Pray about some of these:

Consider your own motives and actions. If you have gone about things in a double-dealing kind of way, ask God to help you put that right.

Think about relationships within your own family. Pray for each person by name. Recall their stories and think about how they have encountered God in different ways. Pray that when their lives are coming to a close, they will be walking with him.

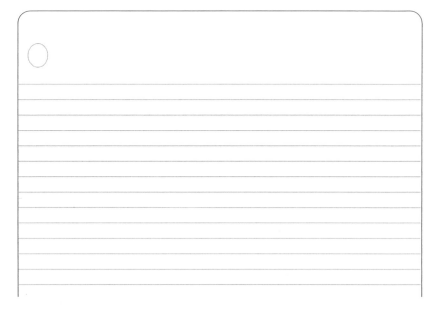

8 Meetings: Jacob and Esau

GET READY

Old political rivals sit down together to talk. A family feud softens over the years, and the protagonists re-establish contact. These are steps towards reconciliation which is at the heart of the gospel.

READ Genesis 32–36

Read chapters 32 and 33, then pause to reflect on the story. Now read chapters 34, 35 and 36 for the final stages of Jacob and Esau's story.

Chapter 36 lists the descendants of Esau and their tribal identities, some of which may be familiar to you from other biblical stories.

INTO THE BIBLE

As you read, try to imagine how you would have reacted depending on which brother's side you were on. What would you have wanted to happen at their meeting, given the sad history of the brothers' disagreement?

What kind of blessing did Jacob demand from God at the Jabbok river? Where do you find 'grace' in these chapters?

What was Jacob expecting from his reunion with Esau? What did he deserve? What did he receive?

After his meeting with God (32:30), Jacob limped on towards Bethel – the place of God's original blessing on his life (28:10–22). Perhaps he imagined that with God's renewed blessing (32:29), all would be well. But things didn't go completely smoothly afterwards. Look out for the times of difficulty and sadness Jacob experienced once back in his homeland.

GOD AND YOU

• Have you ever had an experience like this?

> 'When I went into the room where the group was praying, it was as if God was so real – like he was there, so you could touch him. It was awesome, and it totally changed my view of God.'

Whatever happened when Jacob wrestled through the night with the man (32:22–32), it's clear that he had a very real, tangible encounter with God. And he was changed by the experience (32:28).

• Recall any life-changing encounters you've had with God. How important are experiences like this?

- Jacob's meeting with God comes when he is afraid and distressed (32:7). God's blessing often comes to us at such moments. If you are feeling at the end of your tether now, take time to talk with God about this situation and seek his blessing on your life.

- The blessing Jacob received was no guarantee of a quiet life. Ask God to help you walk faithfully as you face the challenges ahead.

Extra

Turn to Hosea 12:2–6 for a glimpse of how Jacob was viewed by his descendants.

INTO ACTION

Jacob was marked by his encounter with God. Do you feel that you have been marked in good or painful ways by meeting with God? How have you been changed by your experience of him? What might God be challenging you to do as a result? Write down some impressions of those experiences and what you think God might have been saying to you through them.

Reconciliation is never easy. If you need to be reconciled with someone, ask God to help you take the first steps today.

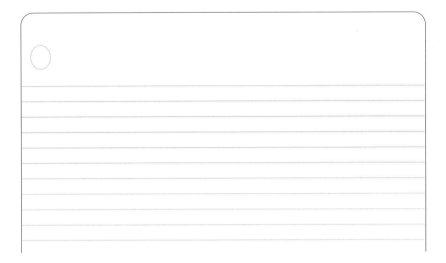

9 Joseph: from prisoner to premier

GET READY

Joseph led a fascinating life. As you read his story, identify the turning points in his life and look for God at work. Maybe God is especially busy in the darker moments of our lives.

READ Genesis 37–41

Read these chapters as a biography of Joseph. You might find it helpful to leave out the story of Judah and Tamar in chapter 38 and come back to it at the end.

INTO THE BIBLE

Few parents would admit to having favourites among their children, but... What emotions would the older brothers have felt towards Joseph? How might they have felt towards their father? Remember, the sons had different mothers. How might this have affected relationships?

In the journal space draw a wavy line across the page and note on it the ups and downs of Joseph's life that you've read about in these chapters.

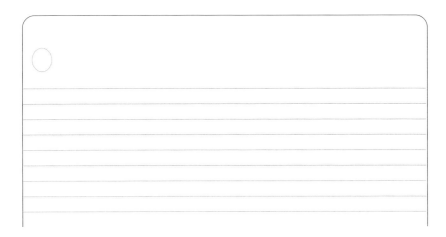

Look at the difference between Joseph, the 17-year-old dreamer (37:1–11), and Joseph, the adult interpreter of Pharaoh's dreams (41:16). What other signs are there in these chapters that Joseph was committed to living under God's authority?

Extra

Joseph's family life is not a major part of the story (41:50–52), but the names of his children will be significant throughout biblical history. Manasseh and Ephraim are granted the status of children of Israel by God and will become tribal heads. God is working his purposes out.

GOD AND YOU

- Think of the incidents in Joseph's life which show he is a man of principle (eg his reaction to Potiphar's wife). For Joseph, sticking to his principles was costly. Can you think of situations where you've had to take a stand because of your Christian principles? How did others react? What happened? Talk with God about any challenging situations facing you now. Pray for wisdom and courage to do what's right.

- Have you ever been unjustly accused, as Joseph was (39:19,20)? How did you cope with this?

- Evidently, Jacob's fourth son Judah was a flawed character (Genesis 38). And he was not the only one of the twelve brothers to have behaved badly. Yet, the name of Judah became significant in the history of God's people (eg Matthew 1:3). Reflect on how God can heal the failures of the past.

INTO ACTION

The young Joseph went on a short routine journey to visit his brothers (37:12–35), but didn't return. Can you imagine the anguish which the news of his apparent death would have caused Jacob? Reflect on this, then spend some time praying for parents who have been bereaved or whose children are missing.

Think of your own life so far. Write down the things you regard as successes and failures. Then write what God has done through each situation or event, and what you think (or hope) he might do in the future. Thank him for his grace and fatherly love.

God used Joseph for the blessing of others. Are you willing and ready for God to use your life in the service of others? Ask God to show you his way forward now.

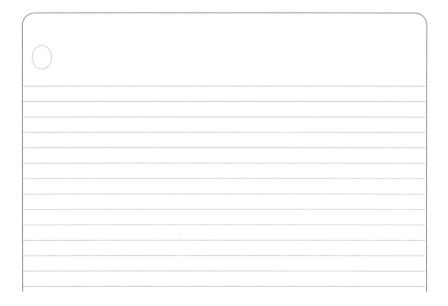

10 Family reunion: from jealousy to joy

GET READY

Family reunions can be a mixed blessing! Long forgotten disputes can resurface and old jealousies can be revived. In this case, the reunion was ultimately happy, and was brought about by a family emergency.

READ Genesis 42–45

Read the entire story in one sitting if you can. Look out for the writer's use of dramatic irony in telling the story. Watch as what the participants know, what we know and what God knows is brought together in the final dénouement. Enjoy the moment of the climax of the story in chapter 45 when Joseph not only reveals his identity, but releases his brothers from blame: '...it was not you who sent me here, but God' (45:8).

INTO THE BIBLE

Genesis 42:6 The brothers come to Joseph and bow down to him. Compare this with the dreams in chapter 37. Was this the fulfilment of what Joseph had dreamt about?

How did Joseph react when his brothers arrived in Egypt? What mixed emotions do you think he would have been feeling as the brothers came before him? They were to return home without one brother (as they had done years before), then on their second visit, Benjamin was taken. Whatever the thinking behind Joseph's actions, there are parallels with his own life (eg the imprisonment of Simeon; Jacob's grief). Look out for them in these chapters.

Genesis 44 Joseph's silver cup would probably have been used for divination – forbidden by God later (Leviticus 20:6; Deuteronomy 18:9–14; Numbers 23:23). The brothers would have known that this was no ordinary cup, and therefore no ordinary crime. Imagine their terror at the possible consequences.

Genesis 45 When Joseph explains all, we catch a glimpse of God's big strategy to preserve the people from whom the Messiah would ultimately come (45:7). The great famine placed the plan of human salvation in jeopardy. So, why did Joseph and his family settle in Egypt?

GOD AND YOU

- You might feel it would have been understandable if Joseph had wreaked revenge on his brothers. Have you ever wanted to take revenge? Why did you feel this way? What perspective on things helped Joseph to forgive his brothers (45:8)?

- How do you understand the Christian command to forgive (Matthew 6:12)? Are there people you need to forgive – or be forgiven by? What about your parents, or brothers or sisters?

- Take a moment to admire and praise God for his 'big picture' plan: Joseph's life and the future coming of the Messiah from Israel's descendants. How do you fit in?

INTO ACTION

Are there broken relationships in your family, or in your church? What could you do to bring about forgiveness and reconciliation?

Extra

Want to think more about forgiveness? Try *Total Forgiveness* by R T Kendall (Hodder and Stoughton, 2001).

11 On the move: Israel to Egypt

GET READY

The final leg of Jacob's journey is approved by God. Even though Egypt is generally a symbol of disobedience to God in Genesis, it was God's plan for the extended family (46:26,27) to move there (46:3,4) They would come back to Canaan, but who could have guessed that it would be over four centuries before this would happen?

READ Genesis 46–50

Enjoy the story as it comes to its conclusion. If you have sons, daughters, nieces or nephews, pray for them as you read 48:15,16.

INTO THE BIBLE

Think of the stories of brothers in Genesis: Cain and Abel (Genesis 4); Esau and Jacob (Genesis 27:1–40); now Manasseh and Ephraim (Genesis 48:12–20). In each case, the younger brother is blessed ahead of the older. Think of the significance of how this upending of convention is a pattern in the life and teaching of Jesus (Mark 10:31; Matthew 23:11,12).

BiBLE
MaX

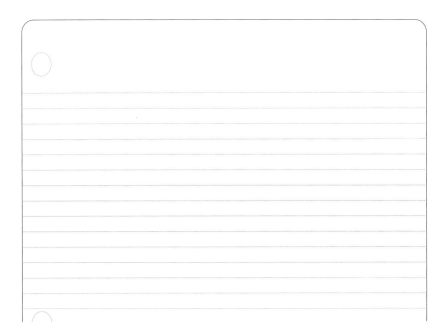

Look out for the clues in each chapter that God's people would return to the special land to which he had led Abraham and his descendants.

Extra

> **Genesis 49:28** The twelve tribes of Israel are associated with the twelve sons of Jacob, but they not always easy to identify in the various lists in the Bible. There are often differences. Joseph almost never appears as a tribal head, but his two sons, Ephraim and Manasseh, are given this status (Joshua 14:4). Levi is not treated as a tribe, but as an order of priests (Numbers 18).

GOD AND YOU

- Joseph and his father wanted to be brought back to their homeland of Canaan to be buried (Genesis 49:29,30; 50:24,25). Today in our mobile, multicultural world many of us have left home and settled in new places. Is 'place' important to you? Where would you like your earthly remains to be buried or scattered? Why was it so important for Jacob and Joseph?

- Joseph looked back on the injustices he suffered as a young man, and saw God's hand in them (50:19–21). Can you see God's hand in the bad things that have happened to you, as well as the good? What effect does this have on your ability to keep moving on your journey?

- Jot down a brief outline of how God has guided you so far in your life. The Israelites would be in Egypt for more than four centuries and then God would lead them to the Promised Land. Where do you think God is guiding you?

INTO ACTION

In Joseph's management of the famine, in order to save lives, he made some difficult and unpopular decisions (Genesis 47:13–26). How can we strike the balance between holding our leaders to account whilst supporting them in the complex task of government that they have been called to fulfil? Pray for your Member of Parliament. You could write to him or her, explaining what you have done. They may be surprised!

BiBlE Max

BIRD'S EYE VIEW

So, you've made it to the end of Genesis! We've read about the beginnings of our world and started out on the journey of God's people. From early on there are clues to the culmination of God's rescue plan through Jesus. Here, in this first book of the Bible, the foundations are laid.

Genesis is also about getting to know God. But we can only know him as he relates to real people. Read the following 'bird's eye view' glimpse of some of the characters we've travelled with through Genesis. As you get to each one, pause to think about and jot down…

> What have I learnt about God from this person's story?
>
> Is there an example to follow or something to avoid?
>
> Who do you identify with and why?

THE GENESIS JOURNEY

Following creation, the Genesis journey begins with **Adam** and **Eve** and their dysfunctional family. **Cain** murders his sibling, **Abel**, and it seems that disaster and pain can be the only outcomes of this tragedy for their descendants.

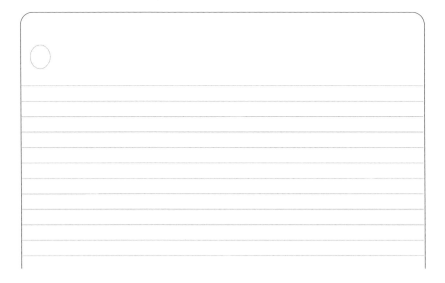

The journey continues...

Noah builds an unlikely boat in the desert and waits for the terrible flood that will swallow the world. With his survival comes a new start, and a new hero. **Abram** is called to uproot from Ur (modern day Tell el-Mukayyar, not far from Basra in Iraq) and journeys to a new home in Canaan (modern day Israel). He and his wife, **Sarai**, make some mistakes along the way, but God's promise to **Abram** trumps his failings. With the new start come new names – **Abraham** and **Sarah** – and a young son, **Isaac**, in his old age. These are testing times since it seems that God's plans for all of us (even today) rest upon **Abraham**'s family, and it's touch and go whether **Isaac** will even survive to adulthood.

Isaac marries the beautiful but ambitious **Rebekah**, who has a favourite out of her two sons, **Esau** and **Jacob**. **Jacob** the younger wins out (by some trickery on the part of his mother). He marries **Rachel** and becomes the wealthy head of the family – and also gets a new name, **Israel**. His sons (and grandsons) will become the tribes of Israel.

BiBlE Max

Joseph, the favourite son, has a dream of a life! The rest of the family travels south to join him in Egypt in search of food in a time of famine. They leave behind the place that God had promised to them. Their descendants won't be back for 450 years, but in that time will have grown in number from the 70 or so who headed to Egypt, to the one million who will leave under Moses' leadership – a nation at last.

GOD AND YOU

- Faith, trust and obedience are big themes through Genesis. What might God be saying to you about any of these?

- Like us, these characters struggled with some massive failings: jealousy, deceit, hatred, family quarrels. Ask God to forgive and help you in areas where you struggle. After reading Genesis, we can know for sure that in God's eyes, failure is not final and that he is a God who keeps his promises.

POSTCARDS

You might like to get some postcards (or Post-its) and write on each one some of the place names you've visited on your travels through Genesis (eg Eden, Ararat, Ur, Bethel, Egypt). You could stick them up somewhere where you'll see them often, then use them as reminders of what you have learnt or prompts to pray – for yourself and others, as you journey with God.

RUTH: A JOURNEY WITH GOD

The Big Picture

The story of Ruth is often thought of as the 'love story' of the Old Testament – but it's so much more. This is the journey of two women and one man whose decisions not only leave an indelible imprint on their own lives, but whose choices also had consequences which have rippled on to affect our own lives today.

The great story of God sweeps through the Bible, drawing people, families and nations into relationship with God and into his great story (Ruth would become the great-grandmother of King David and an ancestor of Jesus himself). In the book of Ruth, we come down to earth and see one displaced family who have already 'survived' heartache most of us can barely imagine.

GETTING STARTED

Read the whole book of Ruth in one sitting – it will probably take you around fifteen minutes. Note any words or phrases that strike you as you read and any questions the story raises for you.

If you already know the plot, don't let that familiarity take away from the pain and the hopelessness these people lived through. Allow Ruth's story to give you insight into your own life. Ask God to speak, challenge, encourage, as you take time to meet with him.

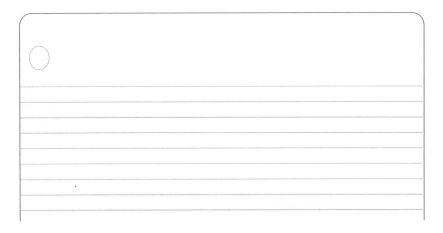

BiBle
MaX

Ruth's story is situated in the time of the judges, during a period of peace between Israel and Moab. The repeated phrase, 'Everyone did as he saw fit', sums up this period (Judges 17:6; 21:25). The picture is of a society that abandons God – yet God never abandons his people. Again and again, they forget God and turn to the local Canaanite gods. Again and again, they are attacked by enemies and cry out to God. There is deliverance and peace for a while until the people turn away from God again. Hopelessness, godlessness, war and poverty were taking their inevitable toll. It was a hard and difficult time (Ruth 1:1).

Extra

Take some time to read part of Judges to gain a sense of the context for Ruth. Read Judges 2; 4,5; 7,8; 13–16. It should take you around fifteen minutes.

THINK ABOUT...

How would you describe the country and times you live in?

What situations, beyond your control, are impacting on your life?

Focus on one or two of the 'bigger' ones. How are you handling these?

A JOURNEY OF GROWTH

Whilst Judges gives the big picture, the book of Ruth shows God at work in the lives of particular individuals to bring about his purposes. It's not just a story of physical journeys but also a journey of growth – from bitterness (Ruth 1:20) to blessing (Ruth 4:14).

Amidst the uncertainty of Ruth's journey, there is the sense of God being in control.

This story may echo some of the questions each of us has at uncertain times: What should I do? Why did this happen? Where is God in this mess? At times, we might feel slightly uncomfortable with the responses of Naomi, Ruth and Boaz – but God's presence is undeniable. Just because we sometimes don't 'hear' God clearly, it doesn't mean that he is absent, neither do difficult circumstances imply an uninterested or impotent God.

Look through Ruth and notice some of the phrases that underline this (eg Ruth 1:6; 1:21; 2:12; 4:13). God may not be involved in a spoken dialogue in this book but his presence is evident.

THINK ABOUT...

How is the Lord in control in your country?

Where are his fingerprints in our world?

How do you think the Lord is in control in your life?

1 Walking in Naomi's shoes

GET READY

From the big picture perspective, let's change the focus and take quite an intimate look at the book of Ruth as we walk in the sandals of Naomi.

As we read the stories in the Bible slowly and deliberately, we begin to see them for what they are. Naomi's story is not a Disney classic – it's a harsh account of loss and abandonment. Let's follow the journey that led this woman from being 'Naomi' to 'Mara' (Ruth 1:20).

READ Ruth 1

INTO THE BIBLE

Ruth 1:1–5 Why had Naomi and her family left Bethlehem? Much happens to Naomi in these verses. Imagine the trauma and devastation of what has taken place.

Ruth 1:6 At last, word reaches Naomi: the Lord had come to the aid of his people and provided food for them. If you'd been Naomi, how would you have responded to the news?

Ruth 1:7–22 As you read, think about the return journey that Naomi is taking. What are the broken dreams she carries home? Notice that Naomi is not alone in her distress. Who are the significant others who are walking with her?

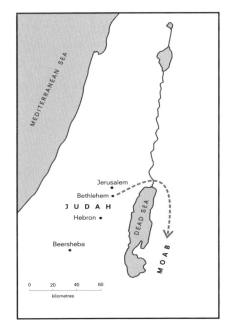

Naomi, with her husband and two sons, left Bethlehem to escape famine and moved to Moab. Years later, when her husband and sons had died, she returned with her daughter-in-law, Ruth (Ruth 1).

GOD AND YOU

- It was many years before Naomi heard that God had come to his people's aid. Has God ever been slow to answer your prayers? If so, how have you handled this?

- Look back through Naomi's journey in this chapter. The hurt is real – the famine, leaving home, the deaths of her husband and sons. Naomi is bitter and empty. What word or phrase best describes you at the moment? Think carefully about this, then the other questions below. Try not to be too self-critical.

   Would people who knew you ten years ago see any changes?

   What changes have taken place (eg work, family, physical, character)?

   How have these changes impacted on you positively or negatively?

- **Ruth 1:8,9** Who has shown significant kindness to you in your life? Or who is showing significant kindness to you at this point in your life?

- **Ruth 1:15–19** Here we see that Ruth is not simply the love story of two people; it is a story where a number of lives impact on each other in various contexts. How does the power of good relationships shine through?

- Are there people you are committed to walk with throughout your lifetime? Who are they?

INTO ACTION

Take time now before God to talk through this commitment. Use this time to make a personal recommitment to those people – and to God too (1:16).

Take time to follow Naomi's example and pray for blessing on each person, as appropriate to their situation.

PS This is not an easy place to leave Naomi's journey. We like a happy ending. But Naomi didn't have the option of skipping on to chapter two to find out what would happen next. Just like us, she had to live one day at a time. Like Naomi, we also have to wait to see where our journey will lead.

2 Walking in Ruth's shoes

GET READY

The book of Ruth asks us not to rush on to the story's ending but to live with these women through their desperate times. Here we find Ruth with no family, no expectations, no security. She faces the uncomfortable prospect of living as a widow in a foreign country. Yet there is hope – in the shape of the kind and honourable Boaz, and in the relationship with her mother-in-law, Naomi.

READ Ruth 2

INTO THE BIBLE

How does Ruth show both her courage and her commitment to Naomi?

How does Boaz show kindness to Ruth?

How does Naomi support Ruth?

GOD AND YOU

- It was early harvest time in Bethlehem (that was around April in that part of the world). We sometimes think of the seasons of the year as reflecting what is happening in our lives. Think about how the season described here (1:22; 2:23) might reflect what was happening in Ruth's life. Which season would you say best describes your own life and relationship with God at the moment?

- Think back to the question in the last section about the people to whom you are committed. In what ways are you providing for them? How do Ruth's actions and her strength of character inspire you?

- Is Ruth a woman to copy, or is she simply a desperate widow clutching at straws? Look out for the difficult decisions Ruth made. Would you have done the same?

- Ruth 'found herself working in a field belonging to Boaz' (2:3). What is your attitude to coincidence? Can you remember some 'coincidences' in your own life where you feel God was at work?

- Ruth was 'provided' for again and again. Look out for how this happens in this chapter, for example: finding herself in Boaz's field (v 3); getting special treatment from Boaz (vs 9,14,15,16). Think about your own life. In what ways are you aware of being provided for?

- Look again at Naomi's words to Ruth in this chapter. Imagine how they would have helped and encouraged her. How have you encouraged friends, family members or work colleagues recently through your words?

Extra

> **Ruth 2:7** There was a law which said that the poor and foreigners were allowed to gather what was left on the fields from the harvest (Leviticus 19:9,10). Boaz went well beyond what the law required (2:16).

- Look out for the 'fingerprints' of God in this story. Psalm 146:9 talks about the Lord watching over the alien and sustaining the fatherless and the widow. How do you see the heartbeat of God working in these women's circumstances? What does this tell us about God?

INTO ACTION

Take some time to consider what you have. We live in times of such plenty that placing ourselves in the shoes of Ruth is not easy. When did you last search for food? Or put yourself in danger to feed your family?

The challenges for us might be:

Am I ready and willing to put myself out for others?

Do I notice the small daily blessings in my life?

Do I acknowledge the goodness which I see both in other people and circumstances around me?

Take some time to thank God for what you do have. Do this without any sense of guilt, but in the joy of blessing, and appreciation of having enough.

Or if, like Ruth, you are facing a difficult situation, take some time to talk to God about this.

If you know someone who is going through hard times, how could you help them practically?

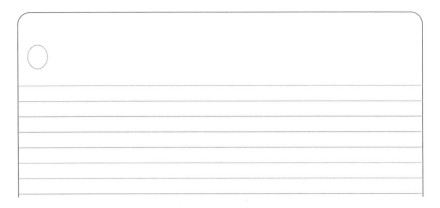

3 Walking in Boaz's shoes

GET READY

Boaz comes onto the scene in chapter 2 of Ruth's story. His story up to that point can only be guessed at. We don't know how he had weathered the famine or what struggles he may have encountered. What we do know is revealed in snippets in Ruth 2–4.

READ Ruth 2:1 – 4:12

INTO THE BIBLE

As you read, look out for everything in these chapters we can learn about Boaz's character. In the journal space, make a list of words or phrases that describe him.

Ruth 3:7–13 The 'kinsman-redeemer' law meant that when a man died childless his next of kin had to marry the widow and raise an heir to him. Ruth, in her actions and words, was boldly claiming this right. But Boaz wasn't the nearest of kin (v 12).

What is Boaz's reaction when he discovers Ruth lying at his feet (v 10)? What does it tell you about his character?

What else do we know about Boaz?

About how old do you think he was (eg 3:10)?

What can you tell about his family background (eg 2:1,3; 4:3)?

What are we told about his status in his community (eg 2:1)?

What can you work out about his character (eg 2:15,16; 3:17)?

Ruth 4:1–12 The city gate was the place where legal business was conducted and the 'elders' acted as witnesses. The closest relative didn't want to take on the extra burden of responsibility for Ruth and any children she might have (v 6).

What do Boaz's dealings with the elders tell you about him? What might they also tell us about his feelings for Ruth?

Extra

Look at the 'fruit of the Spirit' listed in Galatians 5:22,23. How are these qualities reflected in the life of Boaz?

GOD AND YOU

- How do these characteristics show in your own life as you walk with God?

- Prayers, especially prayers of blessing, seem to run through this story. Boaz's first words to Ruth are of blessing (Ruth 2:4). Look also at Ruth 2:12 and 3:10. What can we learn about Boaz from some of these prayers? How do you think they shaped Boaz and influenced the way he lived?

- Take time to think of individuals you know – at work, at church, in your family. Pray for God's blessing on them. How might doing this change your attitude and behaviour towards them?

- Boaz was clearly a man who could 'handle' waiting. He was older than Ruth yet didn't rush to respond to her offer on the threshing floor (3:9), but took time to respond in the appropriate way. Patience and waiting seem to be a recurring theme in this book and Boaz was rich with both.

  Is there anything testing your patience at the moment? Talk to God about this. You might find it helpful to reflect on words from one of the following psalms written by Boaz's great grandson, David: Psalms 4; 13; 27:13,14.

INTO ACTION

In response to seeing how Boaz lived, think about each of these questions:

How can you, as a disciple of Jesus, express godly character?

How do you handle business?

What are your family commitments? How are you handling these?

Can others rely on you to keep your word?

What responsibilities do you have? Are you shirking any of these?

Talk through each of these areas with God. Do you need to change or take action? Ask God to show you how, then pray for courage to take action.

4 Travelling with God

GET READY

The God who is outside of time seems to juggle the present with the future. We watch as God, from his unique place, is active in the lives of two widows in the small town of Bethlehem in Judah more than 1100 years before Jesus was born, whilst at the same time weaving those tales into the greatest redemption story of all time – the impact of which is changing our own lives today.

READ Ruth 4:13–22

…and, if you've time, the whole of Ruth again.

INTO THE BIBLE

What does God do for Boaz, Ruth and Naomi (v14)? Read the genealogy of Jesus in Matthew 1:1–6 and compare this with Ruth 4:18–22. Think about what you know of the names mentioned in the list. What is the name of Boaz's mother (Matthew 1:5; see also Joshua 6:25)? What insight might this give to the character of Boaz?

As you read through Ruth's story again, look out for, and note down, all the clues that God is active in the lives of Ruth, Naomi and Boaz (eg 1:8,16)

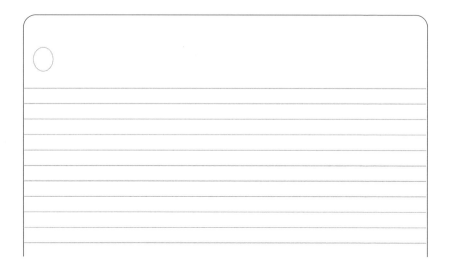

BiBLE Max

GOD AND YOU

- Look back over Ruth 1,2. God doesn't wave a magic wand to rectify times of hardship or severe circumstances. Yes, the Bible is full of the miraculous – but it also seems to be full of the 'extraordinary ordinary'. Ruth's story is like this. Look for it in her friendship with Naomi, in a favourable field owner (who also happens to be a relative), and in the smile and joy of a young baby.

    What does this tell you of how God often chooses to work?

    Are you aware of the 'extraordinary ordinary' in your own life?

    Can you think of times when you have seen God work through the ordinary things of life – either in your own or others' lives?

- **Ruth 4:13–17** God cared for and blessed the individuals in this story – as they had prayed! But he was also working out much bigger purposes through their lives. Spend some time praising God for the blessings he has brought into your life. Now offer him your life and ask him to help you live faithfully according to his purposes.

- What perspective does the genealogy (4:18–22) shed on the significance of Ruth's story? Think about what it tells us about God's activity in our world. What might it suggest about his purposes and plans for your own life?

- The presence of God in Ruth's story is both comforting and uncomfortable. The gentleness with which God transforms the lives of Naomi, Ruth and Boaz is really quite poignant and affirming of our picture of God's love. How is he transforming your life?

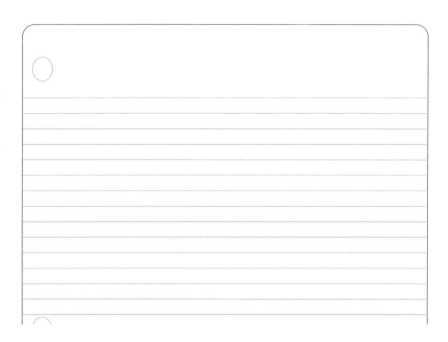

INTO ACTION

Look again at how Ruth lived out her commitment to God (1:16) – with responsibility, hard work, generosity and determination. And God blessed her. You may be going through hard times yourself as you read these words. Thinking of Ruth, how might God be asking you to respond?

Remind yourself of the story of the Good Samaritan (Luke 10:30–37), the outsider who cares for the traveller. Jesus said, 'Go and do likewise' (Luke 10:37). In Ruth's story, Boaz cares for the foreigner and widows. How will you treat the alien, stranger, widow or displaced who have come to your country?

Will you be 'extraordinary' for God in your times? Think of your own family and friendships. What could you do to help bring those around you from being 'Mara' (Ruth 1:20) to a place of blessing?

Think of yourself drawn into the life-changing epic of God's story – it began in Genesis and centres in the life, death and resurrection of Jesus. Who knows where our journey with him will lead? What choice do we have but to love, worship and obey him?

BIRD'S EYE VIEW

THE JOURNEY

The story ends with a husband, a family and a child. It is a remarkable story, a remarkable journey. But Ruth's story is more than just a tale of her personal journey to contentment and fulfilment. Her faithfulness and love reflects God's own faithfulness and love. The consequences of her coming to Bethlehem weren't just for her own life, but had a far greater significance, as Ruth became the great grandmother of King David and an ancestor of Jesus (Micah 5:2).

How does your story fit into God's bigger story? What plans might he have for your life?

SIGNPOSTS

You've looked at some of the detail of Ruth's story, now take a bird's eye view. Think now about any of these themes from Ruth which seem most relevant to your own journey with God.

Patience and waiting

God did not come immediately to the aid of his people (1:6). Naomi had to be prepared to be patient and wait for an answer to her prayer (1:9). Ruth had to wait to find a husband. Boaz had to wait for a wife. Naomi waited for a 'son' (1:11,12; 4:17).

How do you handle waiting?

Blessing

Look again at words of blessing in Ruth (eg 1:8,9; 2:4,12; 3:10; 4:11,12,14).

What can you learn from each of these blessings?

God is in control

This is underlined in Ruth by words which acknowledge that it is God who is in control (eg 1:6; 1:21; 2:12; 4:13).

How is the Lord in control of your country?

How is the Lord in control of your life?

Transformation

The transformation in the lives of Ruth, Naomi and Boaz is quite remarkable.

Have time and people transformed your own experience of 'bitterness'?

Has hope invaded your life?

Has the companionship of others had a deep impact on you?

Has waiting been a big part of your story?

How is God transforming you?

Take time to talk with God about any of the above.

A JOURNEY WITH GOD

Remembering this journey of Ruth and Naomi, think about where you are on your own journey with God. Look at the journey line opposite and circle any of the signs which seem to describe where you are on this journey. You might like to do this with others, then pray for one another.

Look back over your notes in this journal. Take time to pray about any significant areas. Why not make a fresh commitment to God as you continue your own journey with him now?

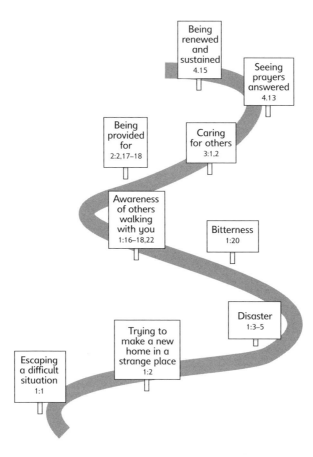

Into a tragic situation the seed of hope is still sown, and the whisper of Jesus is stronger than the difficult things we encounter in our daily lives. God continues to weave beauty into ashes and sometimes, with the gift of hindsight, we no longer see the pain or the scars. What we do see is hope.

'The LORD bless you…' (Ruth 3:10).

More time with God

Enjoyed this title in the *Bible Max* series?

If you'd like to read more, look out for

What's God like?

- Get the big picture of God's story as you read big 'chunks' of his Word.
- 15 more sessions to help you find out more about God as you read about his Son Jesus in **John's Gospel** and learn from **Psalms 1–41**.
- Includes space for journaling to help you reflect and grow as you spend more time with God.

More time with God

WHAT'S GOD LIKE?

£4.99